CHILDREN'S SERMONS

Ready and Rarin' to Go

BY
CYNTHIA DOWNS

COVER ILLUSTRATION
BY
JULIE F. ANDERSON

IN CELEBRATION™
A DIVISION OF INSTRUCTIONAL FAIR·TS DENISON
GRAND RAPIDS, MICHIGAN 49544

IN CELEBRATION™ COPYRIGHT NOTICE

All rights reserved. No part of this publication may be reproduced, stored in a retrieval system, or transmitted in any form or by any means, electronic, mechanical, photocopy, recording, or otherwise, without the prior written permission of the publisher. For information regarding permission write to: In Celebration™ a division of Instructional Fair • TS Denison, P.O. Box 1650, Grand Rapids, MI 49501.

CREDITS

Author: Cynthia Downs
Cover Artist: Julie F. Anderson
Inside Illustrations: Julie F. Anderson
Project Director: Sherrill B. Flora
Editor: David Carey
Typesetting: Pat Geaslor

Scripture from the HOLY BIBLE, NEW INTERNATIONAL VERSION®. Copyright © 1973, 1978, 1984, by International Bible Society. Used by permission of Zondervan Publishing House. All right reserved.

ABOUT THE AUTHOR

Cynthia is married to Edward M. Downs and has five children and two grandchildren. She resides in Stockton, California, and has been a member of the Lincoln Presbyterian Church for more than twenty years. During that time, she has served as an elder and chaired the Fellowship and the Education Commissions. She has taught Sunday School and led the drama program. She wrote curriculum and coordinated a children's program during the church hour.

Currently, she is serving on the Mission/Social Commission because of her involvement as the president of Stockton Metro Ministry. Metro Ministry is an interfaith coalition that works to create a unified voice in the community while serving those who are unable to speak for themselves regarding social issues.

Standard Book Number: 1-56822-540-7
SPCN: 990-219-3366
UPC: 0 13587 23804 9
Children's Sermons
Copyright © 1997 by Instructional Fair •TS Denison
2400 Turner Avenue NW
Grand Rapids, Michigan 49544

All Rights Reserved • Printed in the USA

PURPOSE

The purpose of this book is to provide detailed children's sermons that can be given by any person in a congregation. They are all Christ-centered with the objective of helping the children understand some of the difficult concepts that are evident in the Bible and in a church service.

Just because they are written in a certain format doesn't mean they are set in concrete and cannot be changed to meet a particular style of presentation or worship. They are simply designed to encourage more people to feel comfortable with giving a children's sermon.

Be relaxed and enjoy the children. The adults in the congregation love the children's comments and they will learn from your sermon as much as the children—sometimes more. Be sure to be prepared for some very candid answers from the children and be sure to "roll with the punches."

So, go with God and enjoy. Most of these have been tested and I am here to be a witness to their success. Bless you, for you are contributing to the education of the children in your congregation.

As ever in Christ,

Cynthia Downs

CONTENTS

Thanksgiving 4	God Is Everywhere 20
Christmas (Mexico Story) 5	Honor Thy Father & Mother 21-22
Christmas (Nativity) 6	Jesus Calms a Storm 23-24
Christmas (Baby Jesus) 7	The Living Water 25
Christmas (Baby Jesus) 8	Open Hands & Open Hearts 26
Easter (Keys to the Kingdom) 9	Promises 27
Communion 10	With God's Help,
Evangelism: Sharing The Good News . 11	All Things Are Possible 28
Faith 12	Feelings 29
Prayer 13	Lenten Series: Bread & Wine 30
Resurrection 14	Lenten Series: Crown of Thorns 31
Stewardship (Time, Talent, Treasure) 15-16	Lenten Series: Nails 31
Stewardship (Giving To God) 17-18	Lenten Series: The Robe 31
Children Serving God 19	God's Awesome Adventure 32

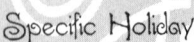
Specific Holiday

THANKSGIVING

Materials

Easel, large paper and felt pens for writing on the paper. Have two columns outlined with CHURCH heading one column and LIVES heading the other.

SERMON

2 Corinthians 9:15 says, "Let us thank God for his priceless gift!" What does priceless mean? (*Encourage responses*) You're right. It means it is so wonderful, that there isn't enough money that could buy it. Do you know of something so special that you can't buy it? (*Pause*) How about the love your Mom and Dad have for you? Or the pets that you love and their love for you? The beautiful sunny days and fun times with friends and family? Can you buy those things? (*Pause*) No, you can't because they are gifts from God.

Thanksgiving is a time for us to say a special thank you to God for all the "priceless gifts" He gives to us. How do we say thank you to God in church? I'm going to write down what you say so we can see all the ways to say thank you. We are going to list things in two different columns, one is how we say thank you in church and the other one is how we say thank you in our daily lives. Possible responses could be:

CHURCH	LIVES
singing	doing what is asked
prayers	prayers
listening to the pastor/teachers	listening to parents/teachers
listening to God	listening to God, etc.

There are many ways that we can say thank you to God and, also, to our parents, teachers, friends and pets. Let's pray.

Dear God, thank you for all the priceless gifts you always give us. Help us to remember to say thank you.

Amen

Specific Holiday

CHRISTMAS (MEXICO STORY)

Materials

> A Mexican Nacimiento (Nativity scene) or Nativity figures that include Mary, Joseph, shepherds, wise men, animals and, if possible, children. The larger, the better.

SERMON

I would like to tell you the Christmas story as it is celebrated in Mexico. It is very similar to ours, but they make their Nativity figures, or *nacimientos*, live the story as it happened. The Mexican people do not just buy a set at the store because every year they add figures to make it bigger and bigger. Many families will move the furniture out of one room so that they can set up their *Nacimiento*. In the past, they used moss from the cypress trees for the setting. Many use a mirror for a lake or river and they have trees and many animal figures because Jesus loved all the animals.

They begin by celebrating *Las Posadas* which is the time when Mary and Joseph left Nazareth and went to Bethlehem for the census count. Remember, King Herod wanted to count all the people, so everyone had to go back to where they had been born. Mary and Joseph, they figured, left on December 16th and traveled for nine days to get to Bethlehem. (*Take Mary and Joseph and put them in the nativity.*)

When they came to Bethlehem, they knocked on all the doors of the hotels, called inns, and they were all full. The Mexicans celebrate by singing a special song called *Letania*, and celebrating *Las Posadas*, which means "The Inns."

On Christmas Eve, all the people go to a special Catholic Mass called *"La Misa del Gallo,"* or the "Crow's Mass." After they get home, they place the baby Jesus in the manger because that was when He was born. The shepherds are added, as are all the children and other animals, to celebrate the birth of Christ. (*Place figures in the Nativity.*)

Way off to the side, the three wise men are placed. They are far away because they came from distant places to see the King of the Jews. (*Place the wise men away from the scene and as you tell the story, move them closer and closer.*) Every day the wise men came closer and closer until January 6th, the "Day of the Kings," when they finally arrived to see Christ. Remember, they brought gifts to the baby Jesus. Do you remember what they were? (*Encourage responses.*) That's right, they brought gold, frankincense, and myrrh. (*Move the wise men into the nativity.*)

The children celebrate the Day of the Kings by leaving hay and water by the front door the night before so that the camels will have food and water as they pass through. The children also leave their shoes there, and if they have been good, their shoes will be filled with treats and candy. Let's pray.

Dear God, thank you for all the ways we can celebrate your birth.   Amen

Specific Holiday

CHRISTMAS (NATIVITY)

Materials

A Nativity scene (it can be in one piece such as an ornament with Mary, Joseph and Jesus) and a doll, or some other toy. A doll is used in this sermon; however, a car or some other appropriate toy would suffice.

SERMON

(*Show the children the Nativity.*) What is this – do you know? Right, it is called a Nativity scene in that it has Mary, Joseph, and the baby Jesus. Why do we have this in our houses right now? It's Christmastime and this is when we celebrate the birth of our Lord and Savior, Jesus Christ. We put the Nativity up to remember the first Christmas, when He was born. How many of you have a Nativity in your house? Great!

(*Show the children the doll.*) Do you know what this is? Yes, it's a doll. When I was six years old, Santa Claus brought me this doll and I loved her and played with her for many years. I had a special bed for her and I dressed her in different clothes and pretended that she was my real baby. Have you ever received something so special for Christmas that you played with it and kept it with you all year? (*Listen and share responses.*)

Now I have a tough question for all of you. Are you ready? How many of you kept your Nativity scene out all year and played with it and kept it with you? Isn't that interesting? Lots of us keep our gifts with us all year, but we put the Nativity scene away for another year and forget about it. We put the reason for Christmas away and don't think about it for almost a whole year.

Maybe this year it might be a good idea to keep a Nativity scene set up and not put it away. That way we can always remember why we celebrate Christmas and why we should celebrate Jesus in every way, every day. Let's pray.

Dear God, we thank you for giving us your Son. Help us to not put Him in a box on a shelf and forget Him.

Amen

CHRISTMAS (BABY JESUS)

Specific Holiday

Materials

A real baby or perhaps items representing a baby, such as a baby book, toys, etc.

SERMON

(*Introduce the baby to the children and let them get acquainted.*) Tell me, what things can this baby do? (*Acknowledge responses.*) Yes, he can cry, eat, dirty his or her diaper, move, smile. What can't this baby do that you and I can do? (*Again, listen and respond.*) You're right. He or she can't feed himself, run, jump, play, go to school, read. (*Try to include everyone's responses.*) Boy, there sure are a lot of things that a baby can't do. Right?

(*Questions to ask the children:*)

- Would you like to be a baby again? Why or why not?
- Why would it be good to be a baby again?
- Why wouldn't it be good?
- Do you think that a baby could change the world?

Well, a baby was born that did change the world. Do you know who that baby was? (*Pause.*) Right, that baby was Jesus. Just think, God loved us so much that he gave up his power and position in Heaven to come to earth as a baby to grow and to live with us. He did this so we could understand him better and we could grow to know him more closely. We're pretty lucky aren't we?

If you wouldn't want to be a baby again, you can imagine how much God loves us to have done just that. Let's pray.

Dear God, we thank you for loving us so much that you came as a little baby so that we might be saved.

Amen

CHRISTMAS (BABY JESUS)

Materials

A baby book, baby shower invitations, talcum powder, baby clothes, etc. in a basket or a bag.

SERMON

(*Show the invitation to a baby shower.*) Do you know what this is? (*Pause for guesses.*) Yes, it's an invitation to a party – a special kind of party. It's called a baby shower. Have any of you ever been to a baby shower? (*Pause; if you feel comfortable, you could ask what they did at the baby shower.*) A baby shower is a way we celebrate with the parents of a new baby. We have a party for the new baby and bring gifts that the baby will need.

What kind of things do you think a baby would need? (*Acknowledge responses and show some of the items that you have brought in the basket or bag.*) Would the baby need powder, or diapers, or oil? (*Pause.*) Yes, a baby needs all of these things and more.

(*Questions to ask children:*)

- If we had a baby shower for Jesus, what would you give Him? (*Acknowledge responses.*)

- Would you want to give Jesus talcum powder, diapers or oil?

- Why would you want to give Him all these things? (*Referring to the basket of items.*)

That's right. We would want to give Him all these things because He was a real baby. He is God but He came to us as a human baby just like you or me. As a baby, He needed everything that any baby would need today. Let's pray.

Dear God, thank you for coming to us as a little baby so that we can be closer to you.

Amen

EASTER (KEYS TO THE KINGDOM)

Specific Holiday

Materials

> A variety of keys are needed; for example, an old skate key, old door keys, key to wind an old clock, etc. Also, a cross that the children can hold; if possible, you can give each child an individual cross as they leave the children's sermon.

SERMON

I'd like to share some special keys with all of you. (*Show the children an old house key and a newer one.*) This key is from a very old house. Look at the key to my house next to this very old one. They sure have changed, haven't they?

(*Show skate key.*) Do you know what this key is? I don't know if your moms or dads would know either, because they probably never used one. Anyone know? It's a skate key. You put your foot on a skate, put straps around your ankle and then you would tighten the skate onto your shoe so you could skate. Have you ever seen an old skate? Do you need a skate key today? No you don't, because now you have shoe skates and in-line skates.

Here's another toughie. (*Show old clock key.*) Who can tell me how to use this key? (*Pause.*) Well, this was a key used to wind a clock. Every day you would have to remember to wind the clock or what would happen? (*Pause.*) Right, it would stop. Do we have to wind our clocks today? (*Pause.*) Today, we just put in a battery, or plug it in, and it works.

There is one key that has not changed, and it will never change. It is called the key to the Kingdom of Heaven. Do you know what that key is? There are several in the church. The cross is the key to Heaven. Jesus died on the cross for us and we should remember that every time we see a cross. The fact that Jesus died on the cross for us, saved us. If we believe in Him and the cross, then we have (*hold up a cross*) the key to the Kingdom of God. Let's pray.

Dear God, thank you for giving us the key to your Kingdom. Help us to always carry your cross in our hearts.

Amen

Specific Subject

COMMUNION

Materials

> A collection of charms on a bracelet. Children love to hear personal stories, so have items that commemorate a special event, person, or place.

SERMON

How many of you know what this is? (*Listen and acknowledge responses.*) You're right, it's a charm bracelet. I have collected charms for many, many years. Why do you suppose these charms are important to me? (*Again, listen and respond verbally by acknowledging certain children.*) For years, my friends and family knew that I loved my bracelet and helped me add to it until I have the bracelet you see here.

This is a ring? Can you guess why a ring is on the bracelet? That's right. My husband gave me this charm to remind me of our wedding day and the ring that I wear on my finger.

This is a baby carriage. Who knows why this one is here? Good! That's my first child, a girl. My other children are represented by the bootie and the pacifier.

(*Continue to go through the charms and talk about the person and/or the event that is associated with each charm. Trips and places visited can be mentioned as well. A charm bracelet is an easy item to use as the charms are symbolic of people, events and places.*)

Who can see some things that we have in the church that are like the charms that remind us of a special person, event or place? (*Identify the cross, chalice and communion bread.*) The cross reminds us of Jesus and the fact that He died for us. It helps us remember the crucifixion and the way that Jesus died.

The wine chalice and bread remind us of the Last Supper and how Jesus told His disciples to always remember Him. Jesus told us that we should drink the wine from the chalice and eat the bread so that we will never forget Him. We call this special time Communion, and through it we communicate our love and gratitude to Jesus, for His life and the salvation that is promised through His death and resurrection. Let's pray.

Dear God, we thank you for all our blessings and we promise to always remember who you are and what you have done for us.

Amen

EVANGELISM SHARING THE GOOD NEWS

MATTHEW 28:19–20

Materials: None

SERMON

I have some questions I'd like to ask you. Raise your hands when you have an answer and I'll try to call on each of you. Okay, are you ready?

1. How did you learn how to drink from a cup?
2. How did you learn how to say your name?
3. How did you learn how to ride a bicycle or tricycle?
4. How did you find out who Jesus is?

There are many people who help us find out things that are important. Raise your hand if you have helped a friend or a brother or sister find out something new? (*Count the hands.*) The question about Jesus and how we found out about him is a very important one because God expects us to tell the "good news" of Jesus and Jesus' love for us. What are some examples of "good news"? (*Listen and share the responses out loud.*)

Here are some examples:

1. A very special program is on TV at 6:00 o'clock tonight. Do you tell your brother or sister about it so they can watch it too? Why or why not?
2. You are a famous doctor and you just discovered a cure for cancer. Do you tell as many people about it as you can? Why or why not?
3. The President of the United States is going to be in your school for only one day? Would you share the news with all your friends? Why or why not?
4. Your mom bought a treat for you and your friends. Would you share it with them or save it for yourself? Why or why not?

Jesus Christ, and what He did to save us, is "good news." Matthew 28:19–20 says: "Therefore go and make them disciples of all nations, baptizing them in the name of the Father and of the Son and of the Holy Spirit, and teaching them to obey everything I have commanded you. And surely I am with you always, to the very end of the age."

God expects us to tell all our friends about the "good news" of Jesus. Do you think you can share the "good news" with your friends, especially the ones that don't know about Jesus and his love? The best way for them to hear the news is if you tell them. Let's pray.

Dear God, thank you for the "good news" of your love and salvation. Help us to share the "good news" with all our friends.

Amen

Specific Subject

FAITH

MATTHEW 14:22–36

Materials

> You will need a large bowl of water and a can of pepper. Hide a small bowl with liquid dish detergent in it. You will need to dip your fingers in the dish detergent without the children seeing you to make this work.

SERMON

In Matthew 14, verses 22–36, the story is told about Jesus walking on water. Raise your hand if you have heard this story before? (*Respond to the hands.*) I'm going to tell you the story again and then I am going to walk on water.

All the disciples got into a boat and were sailing across to the other side of the lake and Jesus went up a hill to be by Himself to pray. At evening time, the boat was in the middle of the lake. Between three and six o'clock in the morning, Jesus joined the disciples in the boat by walking to them on the water. That scared the disciples and they screamed that they were seeing a ghost. Jesus told them not to be afraid, it was only Him.

Peter wanted to walk on the water, too, and he asked Jesus to help him. Jesus told Peter to come to Him and he really walked on the water while he had his eyes on Jesus, but, do you know what happened? Peter looked at the waves and the wind and forgot to keep his eyes on Jesus, and he began to sink into the water. Jesus reached out and grabbed him and said, "What little faith you have! Why did you doubt?"

Doubt means that you don't truly believe and you may panic the way Peter did. Faith means that you believe; when you believe you can, and have faith that Jesus will help you, you can do things that seem too hard. Do you believe that I can walk on water?

(*Bring out the bowl of water and sprinkle lots of pepper on it.*) This bowl of water is the lake and the pepper is the doubts and fears that we have. Who can make the doubts and the fears go away? (*Choose someone to make those doubts and fears go away by making his or her fingers walk on the water. Let others try it as well.*) Do you think I can make the fears and doubts go away? (*Walk your fingers that have the liquid dish detergent on them across the water and watch the pepper move to the side of the bowl.*) The doubts and the fears move away when you keep your eyes on Jesus. Let's pray.

Dear God, thank you for teaching us that you are the way and the life. Help us to keep our eyes on you and follow your teachings so that our faith will be strong and all our doubts and fears will go away.

Amen

Specific Subject

PRAYER

Materials

A chart with the words **Invocation**, **Pastoral Prayer**, and **Benediction** printed on it. Have church bulletins that contain these same words available for each child. The bulletins may have to be specially made; however, it would be more helpful if they were the actual program that the church uses.

SERMON

(*Hold up the bulletins so that the children can see them.*) How many of your moms and dads got one of these this morning? (*Show of hands.*) How many of you looked at the bulletins? (*Show of hands.*) How many of you understand what is on the bulletin or why we have them? (*Show of hands.*)

The bulletins are so that people can find out what is going to happen during our service so they will be ready. (*Pass out the bulletins so that the children can follow along with you.*) Open the bulletins and let's look. (*Go over, generally, what is there; for example, we're going to sing, "Rock of Ages" together. Here's where the sermon is and it's going to be on . . . . The choir's going to sing . . . , etc.*)

Wow, here's some tough words. (*Hold up the chart.*) Who can find these words on his or her bulletin? Is **Invocation** near the beginning, middle, or end? Right, it's near the beginning because that's when we say hello to God and tell Him that we have come to worship Him and praise Him.

Where is the **Pastoral Prayer**? Kind of in the middle, right? This is a time when the congregation comes together to ask God's help for all the people in the congregation or in the church family.

The **Benediction** is where? At the end. Who knows why? You're right, it is a special prayer to end the service and to ask God to protect us and guide us when we're not together.

So, you can see that the bulletin is very helpful and important. Don't forget to look at them and use them to worship God. Let's pray.

Dear God, you give us so many reasons to say thank you. Help us to use all these ways to worship you.

Amen

RESURRECTION

Materials

A list of good news/bad news jokes.

SERMON

Raise your hand if you have ever heard good news/bad news jokes before? I have one for you:

> The good news is that I got one hundred percent on my test at school; the bad news is that it was one hundred percent wrong.

Here's another one:

> The good news is that I won the lottery; the bad news is that I lost the ticket.

Sometimes, when you have to tell someone something bad, it is better to say something good first, that makes the bad news easier to hear. Can you help me think of examples? (*Pause.*) How about, "I really want you to come over to my house, but could you come tomorrow"? That sounds better than saying, "Don't come over," doesn't it?

What if you hear the bad news first? Raise your hand if you like to hear bad news? I didn't think so. Most people don't like bad news. You know, that happened to Jesus' disciples. They heard and saw the bad news of Jesus' crucifixion first, and it made them forget all the promises that Jesus had given them. Remember, in the Bible we read about all the times that Jesus told them that he had to die to save us. Who can tell us what the good news was? (*Share responses.*) That's right, the good news is the resurrection. Do you think that it would have been easier for the disciples to know the bad news of Jesus' death if they had known that he was going to rise from the dead? (*Pause.*) Jesus did tell them, but the bad news of his death made them forget.

> Just think, because Jesus rose from the dead, it was proof enough for many people that He really was God. Also, since Jesus rose from the dead, then He certainly has the power to save us and to help us with our problems. It also shows that Jesus has the power to give us eternal life. Let's pray.

Dear God, thank you for the good news of the resurrection. Help us never to forget the promises that you gave to us so that we can always follow you.

Amen

STEWARDSHIP
(TIME, TALENT, TREASURE)

Materials

> Six one-half gallon cardboard milk cartons covered with white butcher paper. Open the cartons, rinse them out well and dry them thoroughly. Cut down the sides of the four corners to the folded line already on the carton and fold them like a box so that the top is flat. Using masking tape, tape the tops down. Cover the sides of the cartons with white butcher paper. On each carton write one of the following: 1) **Time** 2) **Talents** 3) **Treasure** 4) **Building** 5) **People** 6) **Church**.

SERMON

*(Have the six cartons placed so the names on the cartons are not seen by the children. As you talk about each part of stewardship, put the appropriate carton in it's place. The object is to build a pyramid with the **time**, **talents**, and **treasure** on the bottom, the middle layer is comprised of the **people** and the **building**, and the **church** is on top. (It might be helpful to use a table or an elevated plane so that the congregation can also see.)*

Today, we are going to talk about **stewardship** and how important it is to the church. Have any of you heard the word stewardship before? What does it mean? Does it always mean money or are there other meanings of stewardship? Stewardship means giving, doesn't it? How many ways can you give?

As we talk about giving we are going to build a tower. The first kind of giving, is **Time**. What do we mean by time? It means that you are willing to give of your time by going to Sunday school, church, and other activities in church. You can also give time at home by reading your Bible and praying. You can give time to a friend or to your parents to help them, and the church always needs volunteers who are willing to give of their time.

Next, is **Talent**. Do you have a special talent? Look around the congregation. Pastor _____ uses his/her talent to write sermons, visit the sick and hurting in the church, and to help keep the office and church running smoothly. The people in the choir are using their talents for God, too. What other talents can you find here?

Treasure is the one we talk about the most. It means that you share your money with God in thanks for all that He does for you and for everyone.

STEWARDSHIP
(TIME, TALENT, TREASURE) (Continued)

Two important ingredients of a church are the **People** and the **Building**. The people are you and me and our friends and family. The people in the church reach out with missionaries in far-away countries to help teach others about God. We also help others in our community in many ways. The **Building** is more than just a building – it represents God's house. Not only do we have to pay for the heat and electricity, but through our efforts we keep this building in good condition so we can all worship together.

These building blocks of stewardship all support the **Church**. The time, talent, treasure, building, and people all keep the church together. What do you think would happen if we took away one of these pillars in the church? (*It will fall.*) Let's try and see. (*Choose one child to come and pull the pillar of his/her choice out and watch the tower tumble.*)

What have we learned about the church? We learned that we need . . . what? That's right—time, talent, treasure, building, and people to make a church. This is stewardship. Let's pray.

Dear God, we thank you for giving us the time, the talents and the treasure so that we may be part of your church. Please help us to always remember how important each and every one of us is to your work.

Amen

Specific Subject

STEWARDSHIP (GIVING TO GOD)

Materials

The person giving the children's sermon will have to have four other people helping him or her. All that is needed is an offering plate, a wad of play money, a set of car keys, some jewelry, and two pennies. Have the offering plate situated on an elevated plane so it is visible to everyone.

SERMON

This is a special time in our church – it is a time when people are asked to plan their giving to God and the church. It is called "Stewardship." Stewardship means serving your church and God by helping pay the bills and making sure that the church looks nice, that there is Sunday school, worship services, and so on. There is one catch. God wants you to give with a generous heart. Let's see what God means.

(*A man enters with pockets bulging and goes over to the offering plate. He takes out a wad of money and carefully counts out a few bills and, in a very stuck up manner, drops them into the offering plate and exits.*) How do you feel about the offering given by a person with a wad of money? (*Listen and respond.*) Why do you think he gave what he did? (*Listen and respond.*)

(*Someone else comes in pantomiming driving a car. He or she gets out, polishes a spot on the car, and looks admiringly at it. The actor suddenly sees the children and impulsively puts the keys to the car in the offering plate.*) What do you think of the offering of the car keys? (*Listen and respond.*) Do you think he put in the car keys to please us or God? Is his/her heart a generous heart? (*Listen and respond.*)

(*A woman comes in covered with jewelry and makes sure that the children are watching her. She then puts part of her jewelry in the plate.*) Was her offering given with a generous heart? (*Pause.*)

(*Finally, one childlike person comes in without looking at the children and pulls a penny from one pocket leaving it inside out and another penny from the other pocket leaving it inside out as well. The actor looks at the pennies and puts them gently in the offering plate.*)

Possible Questions:

1. If you had been the person with only two pennies, would you have given both of them to the church?
2. Why do you think the person gave both pennies?

STEWARDSHIP
(GIVING TO GOD) (Continued)

3. Which offering do you think the people in the church would like the most?

   (*Lead the children to the fact that the gifts that would bring in needed money are okay if given in the proper spirit.*)

4. Which offering do you think God liked the most?

   (*The two pennies, as they were given with a generous heart.*)

When we give to God, it is important to remember that the way we give is as important as how much we give. Let's pray.

Dear God, thank you for teaching us how to give to you and also how to give to others. Help us to remember to always give with a generous heart.

Amen

CHILDREN SERVING GOD

JOHN 6:1–13

Materials: None

SERMON

I am going to read a story to you right from the Bible. It tells how important a child can be, so listen for what the little boy did to help Jesus. This is from John 6:1–13 from *The New International Version*.

> Some time after this, Jesus crossed to the far shore of the Sea of Galilee (that is, the Sea of Tiberias), and a great crowd of people followed him because they saw the miraculous signs he had performed on the sick. Then Jesus went up a mountainside and sat down with his disciples. The Jewish Passover Feast was near.
>
> When Jesus looked up and saw that a great crowd coming toward him, he said to Philip, "Where can we buy bread for these people to eat?" He said this only to test him, for he already had in mind what he was going to do.
>
> Philip answered him, "Eight months' wages would not buy enough bread for each one to have a bite!"
>
> Another one of his disciples, Andrew, Simon Peter's brother, spoke up, "Here is a boy with five small barley loaves of bread and two small fish, but how far will they go among so many?"
>
> Jesus said, "Have the people sit down." There was plenty of grass in that plae, and th emen sat down, about five thousand of them. Jesus then took the loaves, gave thanks, and distributed to those who were seated as much as they wanted. He did the same with the fish.
>
> When they all had had enough to eat, he said to his disciples, "Gather the pieces that are left over. Let nothing be wasted.
>
> So they gather them and filled twelve baskets with the pieces of the barley loaves left over by those who had eaten.

Raise your hand if you can tell me what the little boy did to help Jesus? (*Call on a child that has his/her hand raised.*) That's right. The little boy gave Jesus his basket that had five loaves of bread and two fish. Jesus knows that children don't have a lot of money from jobs, or the ability to preach or teach, because they are little. But Jesus does ask you, as a child, to give what you can. It may seem little to you, but look how Jesus can use your little gifts to do mighty and wonderful things. Just like the little boy who gave Jesus all of his lunch, Jesus wants you to give all that you can. We know that Jesus is God's son because He can take even the smallest things and use them in big ways. Imagine, He took five loaves of bread and two fish and fed five thousand people with twelve baskets left over. Let's pray.

Dear God, we thank you because we know that we are important to you. Help us to give you all that we can so that you can use our gifts for great and mighty deeds.

Amen

General Topics

GOD IS EVERYWHERE

Materials

A pretty box such as a small jewelry box and three or more large pictures denoting the earth, space, and the ocean. They could be pictures of an airplane, an undersea picture, or outer space. You could also include a picture of a house and church.

SERMON

(*Show the children the box and, if it is a music box, let them listen to the music and try to identify the tune.*) This is a special box for me and I keep special things inside of it. What special things do you think I might put in my box? Yes, I put my rings in it, and other important jewelry. Do you think I can put God in my box because He's very special to me? No? Why not? (*Listen for responses.*) Right, you can't see God to pick Him up and put Him in a box because He is all around us. Yes, He's too big to put in a box.

Have you ever been in an airplane? Well, do you think God is there with you? I know he's with me. I picture him carrying me and the plane in his hands when I fly.

Is God under the ocean? Yes, he's there, too. He protects and loves all the creatures that live under the water.

Is he out in space? Right again. He created the Heavens and the Earth so we know that he's there.

Is he here in church and in your house? Boy, are you smart. Of course he's there . . . he's everywhere. So, can we put God in a box? (*Listen.*) No way! Why not? Because, God is everywhere. Let's pray.

Dear God, thank you for being s-o-o big and for being everywhere so that we know that we are always safe in your loving care. We love you.

Amen

General Topics

HONOR THY FATHER AND MOTHER

EXODUS 20:12

Materials

A Bible and cards that have the following scriptures on them: Exodus 20:12, Proverbs 22:6, Proverbs 29:17, 1 Timothy 5:8, Ephesians 6:1, Ephesians 6:4, and Proverbs 15:20. The cards should be big enough for the congregation to see and on the back of card 1 should be the letter "I," on the back of card 3 should be the letter "L," card 4 the letter "U," card 5 the letter "V," and card 7 the letter "U." That is so when the Bible verses are turned around, they spell "I LUV U." You are going to ask different children to hold up the Bible verses as you discuss them. When each verse is up, then have the children turn them around so that "I LUV U" can be read by the congregation.

SERMON

We are going to read and talk about some Bible verses that tell us to love our mothers and fathers. They are from *The New International Version*.

1. **Exodus 20:12** says, "Honor your father and your mother, so that you may live long in the land the Lord your God is giving you." What does respect mean? (*Listen and respond to answers.*) That's right, it means that because they are older and because you love them, you listen to them and do what they ask of you. God wants us to trust them to help us and teach us how to grow up to love and follow Jesus. (*Give the card to a child to hold and begin to form a line.*)

2. **Proverbs 22:6** says, "Teach a child how he should live, and he will remember it all of his life." What do you think this means? (*Respond accordingly.*) It means that the things you learn as a child are the things you will always remember and that is why it is so important that you learn the right things to say or do. (*Give the card to another child and have him or her stand next to the first child.*)

3. **Proverbs 29:17** says, "Discipline your son, and he will give you peace; he will bring delight to your soul." Sometimes when we get mad because we are grounded and can't go somewhere or when we get sent to our rooms because we were naughty, we have to remember that our mom and dad are there to make sure that if we have to make mistakes, that we learn from them. They have a big job, haven't they? (*Give the card to another child and have him or her stand next to the second child.*)

General Topics

HONOR THY FATHER AND MOTHER (Continued)

4. **I Timothy 5:8** says, "If anyone does not provide for his relatives, and especially for his immediate family, he has denied the faith and is worse than an unbeliever." Here again, Jesus tells us that it is our job to take care of our family. That means that it is as important for you to be good to your mom and dad as it is for your mom and dad to be good to you. Another big job. (*Give the card to another child and have him or her stand next to the third child.*)

5. **Ephesians 6:1** says, "Children, obey your parents in the Lord, for this is the right." I think this one explains itself. Jesus says that this is His plan to have parents to lead you and guide you and it is your job to do as they say. What do you think? (*Pause and then give the card to another child and have him or her stand next to the fourth child.*)

6. **Ephesians 6:4** says, "Fathers, do not exasperate your children, instead bring them up in the training and instruction of the Lord." In this passage the message is that fathers shold not act unreasonably, but always remember to bring the love of our Lord to our children. (*Pause and then give the card to another child and have him or her stand next to the fifth child.*)

7. Finally, **Proverbs 15:20** says, "A wise son brings joy to his father, but a fool man despises his mother." This is kind of hard. I think it means that God planned it so that parents love their children and children love their parents and when you love someone, you want to make them happy. (*Give the card to another child and have him or her stand next to the sixth child.*)

It all means that God wants us to love one another and especially our fathers and mothers. So, children turn your cards around. It says, "I love you." Let's say it all together. "I love you." Let's pray.

Dear God, thank you for giving us parents that love their children the same way you love all of us. Help us to give back the love that they give to us.

Amen

JESUS CALMS THE STORM

MATTHEW 8:23-27

Materials

> A series of cards are needed. Each card should have a picture and a word for the children to hold up as the story is read. The cards should include a **boat**, **asleep**, **frightened**, **winds**, **waves** and **amazed**. The adult prepares the children and discusses the cards as she or he hands them out to the children. Each child that has a card is to stand and hold up the card when their word is read. Read the story once as a practice and then read it again for final performance.

SERMON

I am going to read a story to you from the Bible but I need your help. I have some cards here and when I read the word on the card, the person that has the card has to stand up and hold the card high so everyone can see it. You see, I am going to be the storyteller but you are going to be the pictures. The first card says **boat**, that's an easy one. (*Give the card to a child.*) The next card says **asleep**. Does this person look asleep? Good. (*Give the card to another child.*) *This* card says **frightened**. That's a big word. What does frightened mean? (*Listen for responses.*) Yes, frightened means to be afraid. Does this person look afraid? Good! (*Give the card to another child.*) This card is **wind**. See how strong it is blowing. (*Give the card to another child.*) This is **waves**. They're really high. (*Give the card to another child.*) The last one is **amazed**. This is a big word for being really surprised or shocked.

You ready? Let's go. I am going to read the story and the ones who have the cards have to stand and hold the card up high when they hear their word.

Paraphrased from Matthew 8:23–27

> Jesus got into a boat, and his disciples went with him. All of a sudden, a fierce storm hit the lake, and the boat was in serious danger of sinking. But Jesus was asleep. The disciples went to him and woke him up. "Save us, Lord!" they said. "We are about to die!"
>
> "Why are you so frightened?" Jesus answered. "Why do you have such little faith?" Then he got up and ordered the winds and the waves to stop, and there was a great calm.

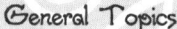

JESUS CALMS THE STORM
(Continued)

Everyone was amazed. "What kind of man is this? They said. "Even the winds and the waves obey him!"

Can you imagine how the disciples felt? To think that Jesus was so powerful that he could stop a huge storm and make it peaceful and calm. You know, there are a lot of times in our lives that seem like a big storm. Do you think that if we asked Jesus to help us, that he could make us feel peaceful and calm, too?

(*Pause.*) I think so, too. Let's do the story again. (*Read the story again with the children holding up the cards. Keep the same children to make it easier.*)

You all did a wonderful job. What great storytellers you are. Let's pray.

Dear God, thank you for always being there in the good times and in the hard times. Help us to have enough faith in you to ask you to help us when we need help.

Amen

THE LIVING WATER

JOHN 4:13–14

Materials

A pitcher of lemonade or punch and glasses for the children.

SERMON

Raise your hands if you have ever been thirsty. When I was a child in the summertime, I loved to play outside until it was almost dark. We played Sardines, Hide and Seek, Kick the Can, and all sorts of games. When I had to come in the house after playing in the cool evening, the house was always hot and I was really thirsty. Have there been times like this when you were really thirsty? (*Share some of the children's stories, helping them to feel really thirsty.*)

This discussion has really made me thirsty. (*Pour some glasses of lemonade or punch and give them to the children to drink.*) What would you think if I told you that you would never be thirsty again? Would you believe me? (*Pause.*) If you were really thirsty, would you pay for a drink? (*Pause.*)

Jesus said in John 4, verses 13 and 14, "Whoever drinks this water (*hold up a glass of punch*) will get thirsty again, but whoever drinks the water that I will give him will never be thirsty again."

What do you think Jesus meant when he said that he will give you his water and you will never be thirsty again? That's a hard question. He is saying that the things of this world are like this glass of water. (*Hold up the cup.*) They never really make us happy or meet our needs for very long. The words and the teachings of Jesus are the things that are going to stay with us forever and ever. The living water. Let's pray.

Dear God, thank you for giving us the living water that is your Love and your Word. Help us to live the way you want us to live.

                       Amen

General Topics

OPEN HANDS AND OPEN HEARTS

Materials

A large bowl filled with peanuts or small candies, and paper cups. Small candies might be more effective to create a "greedier" attitude in the children and, therefore, fuller fists.

SERMON

(Have the large bowl of candies or peanuts available to the children; you are going to ask each child to get one handful of candy, as many as he or she can, until his or her fist is as full as possible.)

I have a bowl full of candy and I want each one of you to have some. You can have one handful, so reach in the bowl and take as much as you can with only one try. Then pass the bowl to your neighbor. (*Pass the bowl to the first child. As the bowl is passed, encourage them to really fill their hands.*) Now, after you get the candy, hold it in your closed fist until everyone is through. Golly it looks like some of the bigger fists get the most, doesn't it? Fill them up. Hold your fists tight. Don't let the candy drop or it's mine.

How does your hand feel when you can't squeeze any more candy in it? Is it getting tired? (*Pass paper cups around so that the children can put the candy in the cup.*) When the cups are passed, take one and put all of your candy in it. Does that feel better? Boy, it sure feels better to have an open hand than a tight fist, doesn't it? (*Pause.*)

If you were a hand, would you rather be an open hand or a closed fist? (*Listen and respond.*) Why is that? (*Respond accordingly.*) What kind of feelings go with a tight fist? (*Pause.*) When you're mad, do you close your hand into a fist? (*Pause.*) What about when you are selfish and don't want to share? Do you grab something into your hand and make a fist? (*Pause.*)

What about an open hand? People who reach out to others do it with an open hand. When you want to make friends with an animal, do you hold out an open hand or a closed fist? (*Listen.*) That's right, you hold out an open hand. Open hands show you're a friend and enjoy things like sharing, giving, being kind . . . just lots of good things. That's why Jesus said that we need to come together with open hands and open hearts . . . open hearts so that we can learn more about Him and open hands of love and sharing. Let's pray.

Dear God, thank you for always being with us and help us to come to you always with open hearts and open hands.

Amen

PROMISES

Materials

A box of cereal that says it has a prize in it or a McDonald's Happy Meal box. Take out the prizes and replace it with a note saying, "I'm sorry."

SERMON

I have a Happy Meal here and inside of it is the new Power Rangers toy that they have been advertising. (*Mention whatever toy is offered at the time.*) Raise your hand if you've ever had one of the toys. (*Pause.*) Does anyone collect them? (*Pause.*) McDonald's always promises to have great toys. (*Choose a child to open the box.*) Open the box and let's see what toy McDonald's promised to give us. What's in there? (*Child should find the note. Take the note and read it.*) The note says, "I'm sorry." They broke their promise. There's no toy. How did that make you feel? (*Listen and acknowledge responses.*)

Did anyone ever break a promise to you? (*Again, respond to answers.*) Did you ever break a promise? (*Listen.*) I need someone to tell me what a promise is. (*Call on various children.*) That's right, a promise is when someone tells you they're going to do something or give you something, just like McDonald's promised to give us a toy. Promises can be good things, but sometimes they can be empty promises when you don't mean them. The missing toy was an empty promise.

I'm going to read some promises and I want you to tell me if they're good promises or empty promises.

1. A stranger says, "Your mother is sick, I'll take you home."
2. The weatherman says, "There will be no rain tomorrow, so you can play outside."
3. Your sister or brother is watching TV and she or he says, "I'll be there in a minute."
4. Just when you get caught doing something you shouldn't, you say, "I'll never do it again, I promise!"
5. A friend says, "I'll be right over after I do my chores."
6. Jesus says, "I am with you always, even to the very end of the age."

(*The children will not necessarily agree with each other and that is okay.*) There sure are a lot of ways that we make promises. Jesus made promises to us and we know that He keeps His promises. You know, I think we should always remember Jesus when we make promises, so that we don't promise anything that we can't do or give. Do you agree? Let's pray.

Dear God, thank you for all the promises that you gave to us and for being a promise keeper. Help us to promise only those things that we can complete.

Amen

General Topics

WITH GOD'S HELP, ALL THINGS ARE POSSIBLE

Materials

A roll of masking tape, a marker pen, and a bag of lollipops for all the children to share, with only one out to use in the sermon.

SERMON

How many of you are good athletes? Good, I'm glad there's so many of you here today because I am going to need a lot of help. First, who can tell me what an athlete is? (*Listen to several responses and elaborate on their answers.*) Tell me, what things can you do best? (*Encourage the children to name different things like running, jumping, etc..*)

Well, today I am going to need people who are good jumpers and we're going to have a contest to see who can jump the farthest. The one who jumps the farthest will get this lollipop. (*Line up about three children and have them jump from the same spot while praising them. Mark where they land with a strip of tape with each child's name on it. Whisper into the ear of the smallest child and tell him/her to just stand on the starting line. Pick up the child under the arms and run with him/her to a spot far from the other marks. With a lot of fanfare, declare this child the winner.*)

(*The children will probably be very verbal about the fact that you helped the small child and he/she really wasn't the winner. Ask the children to sit down so you can explain what happened.*)

Some of you don't seem very happy about the jumping contest. Why is that? (*Listen and comment on responses.*) Well, you're right, that contest wasn't really very fair. The thing that was important was the fact that the one that wasn't the biggest or the strongest could win with some help. It's important to remember that God has promised us in the Bible that all things are possible with His help. We just have to have faith and trust, and to ask Him to help us. Let's pray.

Dear God, please help me to remember when something seems too hard to do, I can ask you to help me and you will give me the strength to do it.

Amen

FEELINGS

Materials

A bucket or pail with a handle is needed. Using red construction paper, cut out a heart the size of the bucket and tape it to the front. Three large stones are needed that will fit into the bucket, with **hate**, **angry**, and **sad** written on them.

SERMON

I have a bucket here with a heart on it. Since I can't show you my heart, or anyone's heart, this will have to do. This bucket is a heart. What do you think someone means when they say that their heart is heavy? (*Take time for responses.*) Well, we're going to find out.

I need someone to hold our heart. (*Choose an older child that can hold the bucket with all three stones in it. Choose a second child to put the **hate** stone in the bucket as you say the following.*) I have a stone that says **hate** on it. What does it mean to hate someone? It means we don't like that person very much and many times we're not very nice to him or her. Put the **hate** stone in the heart. Is the heart heavier? (*Pause.*) Yes, it is.

I have another stone that says **angry** on it. What does it mean to be angry? (*Accept responses.*) That's right. You don't like what someone does and it makes you mad. You know, I have seen fights that were started just because someone is angry. (*Choose another child to put the **angry** stone in the heart.*)

I have one more stone that says **sad** on it. Have you ever felt sad? (*Pause.*) Did you ever make someone else sad? (*Choose another child to put the **sad** stone in and ask the child holding the heart if the heart is heavier.*) Who else wants to see how heavy the heart is now? (*Let another child hold the heart.*)

Wow, our heart is heavy. How can we make it light again? (*Encourage the children to respond.*) Maybe we can take out the stones of **hate**, **angry**, and **sad**. How can we do that? (*Listen for suggestions.*) I have an idea. Maybe we could love someone instead of hating him or her. That would help. Or, we could forgive someone instead of being angry. We could be kind to someone instead of letting him or her be sad. What do you think? Think it would work? Let's try. I love you. (*Take out **hate**.*) I forgive you. (*Take out **angry**.*) You are my friend. (*Take out **sad**.*) Now, how does the heart feel? (*Pause.*) We did it! The heart feels light and happy. Let's pray.

Dear God, thank you for helping us learn why people have heavy hearts. Help us to remember to keep our hearts filled with love, forgiveness and kindness.

Amen

General Topics

LENTEN SERIES

(Each Sunday during the Lenten Season, a mini drama is done to place an item that was used in the crucifixion of Jesus Christ. The central theme is "If only I had known!")

Materials

> Communion bread and chalice, a whip, crown of thorns, large nails (railroad spikes) and material that could pass as Christ's robe.

BREAD AND WINE

(*Wearing choir robes, Mark's mother and Mark enter from opposite sides carrying the bread and wine and stand behind the communion table. After their presentation, they place the elements on the table and exit as they entered.*)

Mark's Mother: I'm Mark's mother. When Mark came to me and asked me if Jesus and his disciples could use my upper room for a Passover meal, I, of course, said yes. After all, Jesus was such a wonderful role model for my son and Mark loved Him so. I made the Passover bread as usual, and it wasn't until later the disciples told me how Jesus broke it and said that it was His body, and with it, we were to remember Him. That's when I began to realize who He really was . . . if only I had known.

Mark: I was so excited when Jesus chose my house to celebrate the Passover meal. My mother baked the Passover bread and I got the wine. I loved Jesus so much that I wanted everything to be just right, so I chose our finest wine. Later Peter told me how Jesus raised the chalice of wine and spoke. I began to realize that this night was different. He said that the wine was His blood and to drink it and remember Him . . . if only I had known what He meant.

Woman: I was walking down the main street when I saw a great crowd of people yelling and laughing. I pushed my way through the crowd so that I could see what all the commotion was about. When I reached the front, I saw that they were flogging a man with the whip that was used for the people being punished for certain crimes. I asked the person standing next to me what this man's crime was. He didn't have much to say, only that He was a Jew and claimed to be their king. I remembered hearing about this man, Jesus, and all the wonderful miracles He had performed, and the people He had healed. Helping others didn't seem like a crime, let alone something that was great enough to be punished in this way. It was then that His eyes met mine and I saw the great love and compassion that shone in them. He actually loved and forgave these people that were whipping Him . . . if only I had known. (*Places whip on the communion table.*)

LENTEN SERIES
CROWN OF THORNS

Roman: You know, it all started when we were told to guard this man named Jesus. Being a Roman soldier can be kind of boring, so we look for fun things to do and when the captain left us with this man, we just started having some fun. It all started innocently enough when one guy mentioned that this guy Jesus was calling himself "King of the Jews." We all knew that there was only one king and he certainly didn't care much for the Jews. One guy said, "What this King needs is a crown." So, he made a crown out of briars and I put it on Jesus' head. Everyone laughed, so I made a big deal out of it. We bowed and I laughed so hard that I thought I would cry. I pushed that crown down on His head until blood began to drip down His forehead and neck from the thorns in the crown. The blood got on my hands and as I was about to wipe it off, I looked into the eyes of Jesus. It was as if I had never seen Him before. The love and compassion in His eyes sent chills over me and I could see that He forgave me even though I caused Him so much pain . . . if only I had known.

NAILS

Member: I'd like to ask for prayers for peace of mind and serenity. You see I haven't been able to sleep much without thinking of the nails. I guess I'd better explain myself because this happened a long time ago. I'm like what you would call a Blacksmith in that I make things out of metal. This has always been a good job and one that keeps me busy. I got the government contract for all the nails that they used to crucify Jesus. I was pretty proud of my work until I went to Calgary to see the crucifixion myself. I was standing there when they nailed Jesus to the cross. I saw His face and the pain is still etched in my mind. The thing that really bothered me was His eyes . . . they were clear and direct and full of love even for the men that were pounding in the nails. Maybe this man Jesus really was the King of the Jews . . . if only I had known.

THE ROBE

Soldier: I am a Roman soldier and I have seen many wars and served bravely without question. It had been a long day and the feeling was really eerie. All the people around were crying and sobbing while they crucified this man Jesus. The other two crosses held two common criminals, but, for some reason, this Jesus didn't seem that common. It's not very pleasant waiting for men to die in such a horrible manner. To help the time pass and to divert our thoughts, we threw the dice. I thought it was my lucky night because I won Jesus' robe. When Jesus died the Heavens seemed to open and I began to shiver. I just can't explain the feeling. It wasn't until I held Jesus' robe that I began to realize the power of this man . . . if only I had known. (*Buries head in the robe and sighs heavily as he drapes it on the pulpit.*)

General Topics

GOD'S AWESOME ADVENTURE
(Vacation Bible School)

(BILLY comes running up to the front of the chancel and faces the children who are sitting against the front pew.)

SKIT/SERMON

BILLY: (*Hand to mouth, calling.*) Sally! Teddy! Hey dudes, where are you? (*Tauntingly.*) I have some awesome news.

TEDDY: (TEDDY *enters.*) Hey Billy! What's so awesome that it couldn't wait!

SALLY: (*Skipping in.*) Woah! Billy, Teddy, gimme five! (*They give each other "five".*) Hey, fellas . . . what's all the noise?

BILLY: It's awesome, that's what! Hold onto your hats dudes, 'cause Lincoln's doin' it again.

TEDDY: Doin' what? Another Eggcellent Adventure? Right on dudes! Woah, that's where I got a whole bunch of friends, right there. (*Talking to the children with thumbs up.*)

BILLY: Boy are you dumb! Lincoln's havin' an *Awesome* Adventure, not another *Eggcellent* Adventure!

SALLY: Okay Billy, what's an awesome adventure?

BILLY: Ya' ready? It's Vacation Bible School! (*Stands smugly with hands on hips.*)

TEDDY: Woah dude, I don't do school in summer . . . I have my guitar, ya' know. (*Plays guitar.*)

SALLY: Boy are you gonna be surprised! It's not really school 'cause it's on Sundays only and during the regular Sunday school time. Know what? I hear it's gonna be a totally awesome *and* excellent adventure!

TEDDY: No way, nothin's more fun than playing my guitar! (*Plays again.*)

BILLY: Hey dude, remember? Your best friend is God. We're gonna learn more about God's awesome love. Hey man, God's more power than . . . than . . . that guitar. I mean . . . it's totally excellent.

TEDDY: Okay . . . I'll go! But you know, I have to ask my mom and dad.

SALLY and BILLY: (*Together.*) We know, you're a good kid. (*Sarcastic.*)

TEDDY: Like, you know it! We're all good kids!

SALLY: Let's go! Let's party! Let's sing, play games, hear stories and do crafts. Billy, will you sit next to me?

BILLY: Bogus! Sit next to a girl? (*Sees* SALLY's *sad expression.*) Well . . . maybe!

TEDDY: Hey Sally, I'll sit by you.

BILLY: Woah, wait! We can't go 'til June eleventh and then it's over August twentieth. Woah, are we lucky cause only grades 3 through 6 can go. Like us . . . how excellent can it get?

TEDDY: I guess it's party time again . . . let's party on, dudes!

BILLY: Like, stand up kids and let's yell. "Party on in VBS" and rock out! (*Have children stand and yell "Party on in VBS" and strum their guitars; everyone hold hands and leave.*)